Lean in Unionized Environment

By Ade Asefeso MCIPS MBA

First Edition

ISBN-13: 978-1508506751

ISBN-10: 1508506752

Publisher: AA Global Sourcing Ltd
Website: http://www.aaglobalsourcing.com

Table of Contents

Disclaimer

This publication is designed to provide competent and reliable information regarding the subject matter covered. However, it is sold with the understanding that the author and publisher are not engaged in rendering professional advice. The authors and publishers specifically disclaim any liability that is incurred from the use or application of contents of this book.

If you purchased this book without a cover you should be aware that this book may have been stolen property and reported as "unsold and destroyed" to the publisher. In this case neither the author nor the publisher has received any payment for this "stripped book."

Dedication

To my family and friends who seems to have been sent here to teach me something about who I am supposed to be. They have nurtured me, challenged me, and even opposed me.... But at every juncture has taught me!

This book is dedicated to my lovely boys, Thomas, Michael and Karl. Teaching them to manage their finance will give them the lives they deserve. They have taught me more about life, presence, and energy management than anything I have done in my life.

Chapter 1: Introduction

The core idea of Lean is to maximize customer value while minimizing waste. Simply, lean means creating more value for customers with fewer resources on the other hand; unionized environment is the process of organizing the employees of a company into a labour union which will act as an intermediary between the employees and company management. In most cases it requires a majority vote of the employees to authorize a union. If a union is established the company is said to be unionized.

What can unions do?

How can modern day labour unions boost their culture for success with the reality of our world today? The truth is jobs everywhere are competing on a global scale. The labour forces that will come out on top are the ones that work side by side with company leaders to put mechanisms in place so that the company and the employees can be successful.

It all starts with leaders. The Union body must elect leaders that are willing and able to lead in manner that will provide a secure future for the current generation as well as future generations. They must demonstrate.
1. A high moral code, professionally and personally.
2. Dedication to fulfilling commitments.
3. Intense professional will.
4. Ability to unite behind team decisions despite personal bias.

5. Basic intelligence.
6. Respect for the brutal truths of reality.
7. Aspiration to be a part of creating the future.

Speaking of the future, unions can work with local schools to prepare the next generation to take their place emphasizing math, science, and technology so companies can have confidence the surrounding population will be able to sustain the business. Not every kid needs to go to University. But every kid should have the skills, knowledge, and wherewithal to support themselves and their future family. Unions can help make that a reality.

Unions can train unemployed or furloughed members on new skills, modern technology, and innovative techniques; not the least of which is Lean Manufacturing.

Unions can work with local, and central Government representatives to attract and maintain manufacturing jobs.

Unions can be active leaders of change in their workplace. Go beyond getting the job done. Strive to increase equipment and team productivity, to simplify systems, and meet challenging goals. As you and those around you contribute actively, you improve your company's ability to compete globally, you improve your community's ability to invest in the future, and you improve your own job security.

A modern labour organization must view knowledge, skills, and the ability to drive innovation as their key sources of power. We all know Unions have power. It's what Unions do with that power that will impact not only the fate of their members and the companies they work for, but that of their community as well.

What is Lean organization?

A lean organization understands customer value and focuses its key processes to continuously increase it. The ultimate goal is to provide perfect value to the customer through a perfect value creation process that has zero waste. To accomplish this, lean thinking changes the focus of management from optimizing separate technologies, assets, and vertical departments to optimizing the flow of products and services through entire value streams that flow horizontally across technologies, assets, and departments to customers.

Eliminating waste along entire value streams, instead of at isolated points, creates processes that need less human effort, less space, less capital, and less time to make products and services at far less costs and with much fewer defects, compared with traditional business systems. Companies are able to respond to changing customer desires with high variety, high quality, low cost, and with very fast throughput times. Also, information management becomes much simpler and more accurate.

Lean for Production and Services

A popular misconception is that lean is suited only for manufacturing and it cannot work in unionized environment. Not true. Lean applies in every business and every process. It is not a tactic or a cost reduction program, but a way of thinking and acting for an entire organization.

Businesses in all industries and services, including healthcare and governments, are using lean principles as the way they think and do. Many organizations choose not to use the word lean, but to label what they do as their own system, such as the Toyota Production System. Why? To drive home the point that lean is not a program or short term cost reduction program, but the way the company operates. The word transformation or lean transformation is often used to characterize a company moving from an old way of thinking to lean thinking. It requires a complete transformation on how a company conducts business. This takes a long-term perspective and perseverance.

Chapter 2: Lean Manufacturing, Six Sigma and Unions Mix?

Lean manufacturing and Six Sigma start with a focus on the process and include methods that require the active involvement of the people who actually do the work. Achieving the benefits of these programs requires cooperation and trust between management and the workforce.

Lean Manufacturing and Six Sigma is a culture of contention between management and a unionized workforce often develops into a perverse lack of trust and dysfunctional behaviour that blocks positive involvement of those who do the work. Addressing this cultural issue is critical before embarking on a continuous improvement program like Lean or Six Sigma.

Companies who have successfully adopted continuous improvement programs with the active support of their union, provide evidence that enlightened management and labour can cooperate to achieve positive results.

Analysis

When starting a Continuous Improvement program, one is exposed to a variety of concepts and methodologies. One core concept is that plant personnel, including any Union members, are critical to the program's success.

First, Focus on the Process

Lean examines the process (value stream) to eliminate waste. This approach avoids cost savings in one area (i.e. "stove pipe") causing higher costs in another area. The objective is to optimize costs across the value stream through a focus on the process.

But, what does "focus on the process" mean? The value stream is broad in scope and is composed of many individual operations. "Focus on the process" involves an examination of the steps in each operation. Steps that do not add value are considered waste and identified for potential elimination. Methodologies like 5S, Value Stream Mapping (VSM), Set-up Reduction, Cellular Manufacturing, Kanban, DMAIC and others focus on the process and help eliminate waste.

Who "Focuses on the Process"?

The traditional approach to process analysis is to give this task to an engineering staff and/or a management team. Their training has given them the skills to analyze and make change; however, they often lack the intimate knowledge of the operational steps. They are located in an office and only observe the process for short periods. Also, changes imposed by engineering are often not sustained. When they return to their office, the operators go back to their old way of doing things.

Different from this traditional approach, Lean Manufacturing and Six Sigma programs involve the people who actually do the work. Included are the plant floor operators, order entry specialists, maintenance technicians, and their associated supervisors. They have the intimate understanding of the process steps and can identify waste. They take "ownership" of the change which sustains improvement and enables compounding of benefits as additional improvements are made.

Enabling the People Who Do the Work to Make the Changes

Lean and Six Sigma provide operational personnel with a proven set of methodologies. One example is "Standardized Work" which defines and documents the operations of workers and machines. Rather than industrial engineering "Work Instructions", Standardized Work represents the real "as is." It enforces consistency (reducing variation among operators) and provides a foundation for continuous improvement.

The operators who do the work create the document and their supervisors review it. Standardized Work then forms the basis for Kaizen events and continuous improvement. As the Standardize Work is improved, the new standard becomes the baseline for further improvements.

An Example of Union Management Contention

Some US companies have history of contentious relationships with their unions. This history started in the late 1930s and has continued into the present time. While the public only reads about it at the time of contract renewal and negotiations, contention occurs daily in many plants as terms of the contract are interpreted and enforced; often with tense disputes. Nearly all participants, on both sides, have unpleasant memories of poor interaction that becomes the basis for a general lack of trust.

Contention often leads to dysfunctional behaviour. Labour can have the viewpoint that hurting the company helps the union member, e.g. enforcement of inflexible work rules provides overtime. Management can view union members as an element of production, not a person with intelligence. Conducting a meaningful Kaizen event, with operators and management, in such an environment borders on the naive and is highly unlikely to lead to real, sustainable improvement.

Unions Can Help

Some unionized plants have successfully adopted continuous improvement programs with positive results. One example is a automotive spare part manufacturer client of ours in the UK. This site has over 1,000 employees including 600 union members and it's a prime contractor for major European auto industry.

They started their continuous improvement program in 2000. Three key constituencies came together to give their Lean Manufacturing program a strong start. One, their prime customer, Toyota, was ramping-up their requirements and supported Lean to improve production. Two the company had a few new senior managers that where familiar with Lean Manufacturing. Three, enlightened Union leadership approached management offering their help as part of an effort to keep the jobs local.

There Lean Manufacturing program has, at its core, a focus on cultural change that treats the people who do the work with respect and integrity. The mind set transitioned from "entitlement" (not my job), to "activity" (look busy), and then to "results" (achieve the objective). Union leadership is a key member and facilitator of this shift in culture. Overall, there has been a 44% reduction in inventory. They were able to increase production by 50% within the same floor space; meeting the requirements of their key customer and, the union is happy because outsourcing was prevented and their jobs stayed local.

Food for Thought

Adopt Lean Manufacturing and Six Sigma with a focus on the process as a means of improving productivity. Involve the people who actually do the work and encourage an environment of mutual respect. Bring them into the continuous improvement program as full participants. Then trust all of your people and engage their brains.

16

Chapter 3: Unions Work Only If Management Doesn't

The employer that has an honest, well intentioned and decent attitude toward his employees has a foundation that will make union organizing of his business entity unlikely. If the employer successfully addresses issues that cause employees discomfort, unrest or alienation, the employer becomes a difficult target for union organizers. Preserving a union-free workplace is an honour in today's world of pressured loyalty and broken trust.

It is noble for a management team to maintain a direct relationship with employees because whenever disputes occur in unionized shops, the ultimate victims are the employees; the members of the union. They are the ones who put it all on the line during a labour dispute. They are the ones who forfeit pay and benefits during a strike. They are the ones who are subject to the divisiveness and sometimes terroristic behaviour of their co-workers or outside union organizers who impede their ability to earn a livelihood. The employer who preserves a union-free status has protected his employees and their families.

The cost of running a unionized shop has been estimated to be 25 percent to 35 percent higher than a non-union operation. These costs do not reflect higher wages and fringe benefits that are paid to unionized employees.

We did some work with a major manufacturing company that runs 20 manufacturing plants; half of which are union free, the other half unionized, at least in part. We found that the administrative budgets of the unionized plants were 30 percent more than in the non-unionized plants. In the unionized plants, the human resource staffs were larger because they needed people to handle grievances, job descriptions, rate negotiations, time and motion measurements, and compliance with government regulations. The union-free facilities were not as inclined to have "bird dogs" overseeing compliance with many of the workplace statutes.

One of the costs of dealing with the union relates to a higher frequency of involvement with outside regulatory agencies, especially those dealing with hours and wages. Some of the indirect costs of dealing with unions relate to outside services. Most manufacturing operations today buy legal counsel on an as-needed basis. The need for a labour lawyer or other professional to handle contract negotiations, administer the contract as it relates to grievances and arbitrations and to preview compliance with the collective bargaining agreement are expensive propositions. Virtually none of those costs exist in a union-free operation.

Unions will advertise that 97 percent of all labour agreements are settled without a strike. What they neglect to say is that roughly 50 percent of initial contract negotiations never end in an executed collective bargaining agreement. Moreover, more than 75 percent of negotiations related to a first contract are not concluded within one year of the election, according to the Federal Mediation and Conciliation Service. Certainly, the employees are frustrated during that period because when they reached out to the union they did so with the prospect that something would change; that work and pay conditions would be better as a result of representation by the union. If their hopes are dashed or at least stalled for over a year, their frustration level is exceedingly high.

In such a situation, the direct costs to the business are lost productivity, higher employee turnover, absenteeism and perhaps even sabotage. The indirect costs often relate to the corporate campaign tactic that unions are so apt to employ.

It is quite common when negotiations do not result in a quick contract that unions will file unfair labour practice charges, accusing the employer of bad faith bargaining or other unlawful practices, all of which come with the cost of a defence. How much do these tactics cost? The answer depends on the employer, the union, the issues and what flaming radical the employer is likely to have assigned to investigate his unfair labour practice from the regional office of the National Labour Relations Board.

Another hidden cost of dealing with a union is lost flexibility. Contracts do not improve the employer's ability to move fast, and in today's rapidly changing world he who hesitates loses. Work rules and other contract language that spell out rigid operating guidelines don't assist an employer in responding to the pace of change today. Nobody wants to have to decide whose turn it is to work overtime or to restrict the supervisor from helping out in a situation that could be resolved in seconds with a couple of additional helping hands. Employees don't like those situations either. Most employees want to do the right thing, and they know that anything impeding their employer's ability to be successful ultimately represent a job security threat to them. Often times you will hear employees say, "I wish we didn't have to deal with this union situation."

Employees want to participate in decisions. Employees are seeking a voice, dignity, respect, protection from a changing world and some assurance that further pay cuts and benefit changes will cease. While a union cannot guarantee any of those wishes, employees will often reach out to the union if they feel their situation is hopeless. There is considerable evidence that employee-involvement programs inhibit union organizing, both by reducing union win rates in certification elections and by preventing unions from even mounting campaigns.

In studying 200 union organizing campaigns beginning in 1994 and surveying many organizers, Bronfenbrenner found that unions won 48 percent of the time when there were no employee involvement programs and only 30 percent when there were such programs.

Employee involvement programs coupled with other power-sharing programs like alternative dispute resolution systems, give employees a sense that they control their destiny within the workplace. Those processes are not normally available in a unionized operation because the union wants to be the gatekeeper of that power. When employees become part of a union, they give up the right to control their own destiny.

Experience shows that when employees are advised that participation programs would be modified or eliminated if the union came in, employees who participate in these programs often become the staunchest anti-union spokesmen for the company.

Chapter 4: Where Do We Begin Lean in Unionized Environment?

The same place we would regardless of whether we have union or non-union plants.

First, the company's senior leadership team should initiate the strategy and prepare the template for broad communications of the strategy and the forever commitment it takes.

No longer will the hourly employees be asked to check their brains at the time clock and pick them up on the way out.

Let me say that another way. It is a career-long commitment for all current and future employees, not a flavour-of-the-month that is now in vogue but will change with the next new idea. (This is the first step of the process that far too often is a hurdle the senior leadership team isn't committed enough to jump. This, of course, is the principal reason why most so-called "initiatives" fail.)

Once the corporate strategy is agreed to by the senior leaders and the board of directors, then the senior leaders go into execution mode.

Almost always in a manufacturing company the initial priority is to start on the shop floor. Why? Because manufacturing operations have most of the people and spend most of the money! The shop floor is where the most low-hanging fruit is and, typically, where enormous improvement opportunities are found.

First a senior leader, ideally the CEO, distributes an official communication on the Continuous Improvement (CI) journey, the senior leaders and board approval and the commitment that is been made. I recommend this take the form of an electronic audio/visual communication. The CEO can then make it clear that the overall strategy is for an enterprise-wide drive for excellence that includes all functions and all locations and that manufacturing is where we will start and pull other functions in at the appropriate time.

If the factories aren't noticeably moving the needle on performance improvements in the first two years, senior leaders will either lose interest or start replacing people.

In the meantime, all functions are expected to provide the necessary response that manufacturing requires to resolve issues in the shops in the context that it is in support of the company's No. 1 priority.

There are, of course, more modern ways for the CEO to do this initial communication, but back in the '90s, and because we had such a broad geography of locations to receive the message, recording a video of the CEO and the CI message was our best approach. That way the CEO could address all employees in a personal way, anywhere in the world, and get the common message out quickly.

The site leader, regardless of function, would show the video and then "localize" what that meant to their specific site. It's a great time to give everyone time to think about the anticipated changes that are being suggested, e.g. more holistic training well beyond how to do their specific job; training on proper use of the lean toolset; understanding the culture change that the company seeks and the new expectations regarding hourly employee involvement, etc.

The manufacturing, engineering, quality, materials and scheduling, HR, maintenance, accounting functions begin to detail the specific priorities that will be tackled and resourced to significantly improve performance. The plant manager, with HR assistance, will be leading the frequent communications and training necessary to quickly develop the staff team and first-line supervisors so they are ready to begin engaging with hourlies in a different way.

Corporate leaders have made the commitment and local leaders, including the union, are expected to execute the strategy with no excuses.

This should be among the top priorities for the plant manager.

But make no mistake. If the factories aren't noticeably moving the needle on performance improvements in the first two years, senior leaders will either lose interest or start replacing people. Senior leaders losing interest because they can't find the results of their investment in CI on the income statement, the balance sheet or customer service reports is the second most common reason for CI going into the side ditch.

If the results aren't there, then it's reasonable to ask why not? Or, why are we doing this?

The better response, which in my opinion is far too rare, is for senior leaders to bow their necks and repeat their COMMITMENT to CI and start weeding out the leaders who aren't leading in that fashion and think the necessary changes don't apply to them. Absent that, the company's CI plans are already doomed. Senior leaders don't have a vote at this junction. It's time to get on board and help lead the change or go work somewhere else.

Where Do Unions Fit In?

Now to the union part. Just prior to the "all hands on deck" presentation by the CEO to all employees, the plant manager should have a short meeting with the local union reps and give them a heads up as to the content of the CEO's upcoming remarks. Ask them to be open minded as we start the journey and ask that they join us in supporting this number one priority of the corporation.

Most importantly, begin the dialog on why the journey to sustained excellence is so important to the company's future and to the plant's future as well. Emphasize its importance in helping the plant sustain and grow jobs in the community, i.e., the job-security card.

Tie in the need to be competitive globally with the products made there and that maintaining the status quo ultimately leads to competitive/survival issues. We are either getting worse or getting better; there is no standing still. Unless the specific plant is already on the "to be closed" list, then there is hope; but they have got to get going and fast!

Involve Everyone in Helping to Improve the Operation.

Also critical is to explain and discuss the intended culture change of involvement and for management to be more responsive to the needs of hourly people and the machine operators in particular. Pledge that your management team is there to serve and to help eliminate all the reasons why operators have a bad day, e.g., wrong operating instructions, errors in the bills of material, inadequate training, material supplier issues, poor maintenance, etc.

The biggest one of all is to involve everyone in helping to improve the operation. No longer will the hourly employees be asked to check their brains at the time clock and pick them up on the way out.

Create Positive Momentum

The new culture will seek to take full advantage of their experience, expertise and to solicit their ideas. (The urgency for different behaviour by the leadership is critical. Nothing can kill interest faster than making this commitment and then supervisor and manager behaviours and attitudes towards hourlies don't change. This is the third leading cause of failure.)

The leader must create urgency, with high energy and elevated expectations. While people are expecting change, don't disappoint them! The first 6 to 12 months will be critical to creating positive momentum.

Also, repeat the message to all who hesitate or openly resist. There will be no vote on this. All facilities, all functions will be participating. Corporate leaders have made the commitment and local leaders, including the union, are expected to execute the strategy with no excuses.

Chapter 5: Using Monetary Incentives to Drive Continuous Improvement

This is often one of the more controversial and hotly debated topics with companies striving to achieve and sustain excellence. There is certainly no right or wrong answer here, but I am happy to share my personal experience with this dilemma. There are company and facility specific set of circumstances that must be understood before embarking on monetary incentives for a large universe of new participants.

First, let's agree that whether we call it pay for performance (P4P), gain sharing, group incentive or whatever, that the essential ingredient here is to design a compensation scheme that makes the hourly associates' compensation variable subject to actual performance vs. a predetermined set of objectives.

Often these designs also include salaried folks as well who do not participate in any corporate management incentive program. (Anyone who does participate in a corporate incentive program is excluded from a P4P. No double dipping!)

Rather than go into the mechanics of a system design, I'll address some of the considerations involved, which are formidable. If you have the right climate in place to entertain the notion of gain sharing then there are experts you can partner with to lead your company through the design process.

Considerations

1. Have you been on the continuous improvement journey for at least five years? This is important because the culture change on the shop floor takes time, and it must be far enough along that hourly folks are well educated/trained in how to think about their work, how to use the basic lean toolset for problem-solving and be in control of their own work processes. They must also be equipped to see the linkage between what value they add and the benefit to customers and shareholders and their own job security. If these basics are not well established, you are not ready to talk about radical compensation redesign.

2. Does your management from the CEO on down understand the commitment that is being made to sustain such a program? If they don't understand or are not interested in understanding, forget about it. Reneging on a program such as this will set you back, if not kill, your continuous improvement (CI) program as it will shatter whatever level of credibility and trust other leaders have worked so hard to create.

3. Are your facilities union or non-union? I've had a few modestly successful P4P programs in both environments, but the "pilot" program should be in a non-union plant, if possible. It's simply easier to engage directly with hourly people, learn from mistakes and not have a middle man involved until a basic design is made and a successful pilot has been completed. In addition, it is typically a harder selling job to the unions because it requires change in their basic mindset relative to negotiations. P4P is NOT an entitlement program! Improved performance is measured net of inflation and is tied to business performance. If the company has a bad year, then chances are the individual plants won't be paying fat P4P bonuses.

4. What factors will be included in the P4P calculations? Will PPV (purchased material price variance to standard) be included/excluded? Will sales price changes in the marketplace be included/excluded? Will GWIs (general wage increases) continue or be eliminated or reduced in favour of more variable compensation via P4P?

5. P4P programs are just that. Leadership must make the linkage clear between shop-floor results and corporate productivity improvements. For example, if the corporate objective is to increase operating margin (OM) by $X\%$, then how much of that should be tied to market pricing vs. product mix vs. factory productivity? It's a non-start in the plants if things they have absolutely no control over start affecting their ability to meet plant objectives. On the other hand, if a major vehicle to improve OM depends on incremental sales growth of particular products groups, then an appropriate plant objective might be "improve Overall Equipment Effectiveness (OEE) on constrained machine XXX by 10 points from 75% to 85% in order to meet additional demand being brought in by the sales group."

This is how you get aligned objectives top to bottom. If the plant meets their 85% OEE goal but the sales team doesn't bring in the additional business, will this affect the P4P payout? These and many other scenarios must be anticipated and played out during the planning process to minimize the surprises along the way. This is why doing a one facility pilot is so crucial. If P4P turns out to be a non-starter, then at least it's on a scale that is quite manageable to unwind.

6. Are you prepared to meticulously track the metrics so that you can report with confidence at the monthly, quarterly and annual employee update meetings and be completely understood? When the news is bad will hourly associates understand and accept the news? Will there be job actions if failure to have regular payouts persists? Also keep in mind that if you start this variable compensation system, the record keeping must be above reproach or once again the lack of trust and credibility will be deadly to your CI future.

7. Rather than thinking about P4P as a "corporate program," instead, think about it one facility at a time. Even in a world-class company there are often facilities that are not yet world-class. Any plant that gets the opportunity to pursue a P4P is selected based on their status as already being one of the best in the world at what they do and how they do it.

Few Candidates for Broad-based P4P Scheme

At the end of the day there has to be a win-win-win process. Customers have to win with higher quality, competitive cost, superior delivery performance and customer service. Shareholders have to win via improved returns on investment based on continuously improving results. Employees have to win by sharing in the company's success based on their positive contributions to an improving business.

Will hourly associates be better off continuing to receive a cost of living increase or will they be better off because they have a chance to earn significantly more in a good year? Can they accept that some years their compensation will be only their base rate since no incentive pay was earned?

There is an extraordinary number of moving parts here. My opinion is that very few companies are candidates to pursue a broad-based P4P scheme. Why? Because the disciplined thinking, meticulous attention to detail required to manage the processes over a long period of time, the long-term leadership commitment and the extraordinary communications that are critical to sustaining such a process are formidable but absolutely necessary.

Since so few companies that start the journey to excellence are still on the journey after 10 years, I did submit that there is a pretty small universe of entire companies that should be burning a lot of calories worrying about a formal P4P program.

On the other hand, it's likely that there are many more companies out there where a few plants might be worthy of consideration. Even then, in my opinion, it's a high risk commitment over the long haul, and you should always define the conditions under which the P4P program will be given last rites so it's clear to all from the beginning. Having a long-term success with P4P is a long, downhill putt.

Chapter 6: Can Employee Resistance Be Transformed to Buy-in?

The short answer is an emphatic "Yes." There are many and varied reasons why Lean initiatives fail to launch well, stall in implementation, or die on the vine rather than flourish in sustainment. But in my experience as a Lean practitioner and organizational change consultant, there are a few keys to successful introduction and implementation. These are pointed directly at engaging employees in the process early and often to foster their understanding, and ultimately, their commitment to contributing to Lean success.

Meaning Matters. Sometimes the word "lean" itself can have a negative connotation; especially if the organization has a history of outsourcing and/or routinely cutting jobs to reduce costs. "Lean" can often sound as if it is an action word meaning, "Let's get lean and do more with less." It's no wonder that employees and labour leaders in unionized environments hear the word "lean" and tune out, shut down or brace for battle. This is where a comprehensive educational introduction is critical in fostering understanding of the concepts behind Lean and its purpose.

It's also critical that leaders help employees understand how their work matters to overall outcomes. That is where the Lean Daily Management

System (LDMS) is so critical to creating employee buy-in. In an automotive spare part plant where I worked, the LDMS process included 10-minute meetings at the start of every shift so that team members could review the prior day's performance on Key Performance Indicators like production, quality and safety. The use of a visual team board helped the group see performance trends, and connect the dots between their results and that of the overall plant. They talked about the opportunities and demands of the upcoming shift, and had the opportunity to offer suggestions, raise concerns and questions, and ultimately, to leave the meeting well-informed about the plan for the day, and their role in it.

Cut to the Chase. Talking about Lean without addressing employee concerns and fears is wasted breath. The leading concern about Lean among employees typically relates to job loss, so leaders need to address the issue head-on. If management is willing to commit that no job loss will result from Lean implementation, that news is sure to attract employees' (and union leaders') attention in positive ways. In the automotive manufacturing plant I referenced, management made a verbal commitment to that effect, and it created an opportunity for employees to consider Lean on its merits, without the baggage of misinformation and fear of job loss. In that facility, which was unionized, having labour leaders understand Lean concepts and purposes went a long way in asking for their help in explaining it to their members.

Hearing not Telling. Lean is designed to reduce the seven "deadly forms of waste." Reducing each of these defects, overproduction, over processing, wasted motion, inventory (work in process), transport/handling and waiting; simply makes a facility better. Most employees have complained about these forms of waste for years, only for the complaints to fall on deaf ears. To create employee buy-in for the Lean process and to exponentially improve returns on the Lean investment, leaders should strive to practice the art of listening and assure that their Lean process creates mechanisms for employees to give meaningful input into improvements. As the people who do the work every day, employees know it best and assuring their expertise is effectively heard and acted upon is critical. Success with Lean is about helping employees understand that it's a process that happens with them, not to them.

What's In It For Me? With the introduction of any change, everyone from the C-suite to the shop floor, naturally ask, "What's In It For Me?" (WIIFM.) It's not an unfair question. One way to get at the answer is to ask any supervisor or employee on a production line what constitutes a good day. Most of them would say it's when the operation is smooth, when components show up on time and the machinery is running well. That is exactly what Lean helped create on the automotive plant's production line through the use of Kanban, a simple signalling system that notified operators when production quotas had been met so they could assure they were only producing what was needed and at the time it was needed. This resulted in a 25 percent reduction in the waste associated with over-production, and enabled operators to shift their time and attention to value-added tasks like preventive maintenance, housekeeping (to prevent waste associated with product contamination), kaizen process improvement projects, etc. It gave the operators greater flexibility in work tasks (which humans inherently desire), and enabled supervisors to devote their time and attention to coaching team members, rather than "putting out fires," searching for in-process "stock" that ran out prematurely due to the over-production, or trying to locate space for storing over-produced treads that weren't needed in the next manufacturing step.

The Big Picture. In addition to understanding how Lean affects them personally, leaders need to assure employees also understand the business rationale for the change. The simple message of, "The only way to survive in (any) market, is to get better; to constantly improve" is logical and resonates with employees' sensibilities. A friend of mine once said "In my two decades as a member of the United Steel Workers of America, I came to understand that job security is not a function of a labour contract. No company can have language in the collective bargaining agreement which guarantees employment for the next 30 years. Real job security comes from being better than the competition, and that is where Lean is a process to be embraced rather than shunned."

My emphatic "Yes" to the question of "Can Employee Resistance to Lean Be Transformed to

Buy-In?" hinges first on a few core communication principles.

1. Give meaning to the need for change on a personal and organizational level and assure employees understand how their efforts contribute to operational performance.

2. Address employee concerns and fears in a straightforward manner, with sincere commitments about what happens and doesn't happen when Lean reduces waste.

3. Make employees central to Lean by soliciting their improvement ideas, tapping into their expertise in implementation, and continually gathering and listening to their feedback on how processes are working and can be improved further.

Applying these principles will not only minimize initial resistance to Lean, it will create high levels of commitment from employees who recognize that as they gain personal satisfaction from having meaningful involvement in workplace improvements, they also have a vested interest in helping achieve organizational success through a well-executed Lean initiative and that is a win-win worthy of an emphatic "Yes!"

Chapter 7: Lean Continuous Improvement Requires Servant Leadership

Lean Continuous Improvement is a service program and should be dedicated to elevating the minds and talents of everyone within the organization.

I was educated and trained that Lean Continuous Improvement is a philosophy centred in service; so much so, that if a process failed, you (as leadership) were to apologize to the employee and solicit feedback and ideas about how to make it successful.

It was taught that everyone was obligated to not only supply the employee with efficient, repeatable processes but also to encourage the employee in Lean Continuous Improvement Thinking.

The encouragement to get everyone on board with the continuous improvement philosophy was more important than quickly "kaizening" to save money. Saving money was important, but it also was understood that the time spent cultivating the culture would in the long run yield results by everyone instead of results by a few. A friend of mine always say, "Instead of 10 or 20 eyes on waste, we want 300 eyes on waste." Wow. That makes sense.

Some organizations have lost sight of this and focused on immediate satisfaction through saving money quickly at the expense of the people and the culture. If this is your organization, then I hope this chapter might reignite the fire of service.

Serve the people, invest in the people. The company will grow as the minds grow.

True lean continuous improvement requires a servant leader attitude and outlook to be successful within an organization. Lean continuous improvement (in its purest sense) actually demands that leadership support others in their development. Hence, rather than exercising power over the people, the power should be shared with the people by putting their development needs first.

Let's look at the word service.

Service has multiple definitions. I am going to use three key ones.
1. The action of helping someone.
2. A system supplying a need.
3. Perform routine maintenance on (something).

We will start with "the action of helping someone." The action of helping is to make it easier for someone to do something. It is essentially to provide one's services or resources to someone in need. In a continuous improvement sense it is to provide a person with not only the materials but also the time necessary to operate effectively.

The act of helping someone is not just sending an expert to improve a process or removing an ergonomic risk from an operation via kaizen. It's not just writing standard work for them or displaying work instructions visually.

All of those elements are good for the employee, yes. But it is just as important, just as vital, to send that expert out to train, influence and engage the individual. Helping most certainly means to improve the process, but equally it communicates the need to invest in the knowledge and experience level of the employee.

In the continuous improvement realm it means to help every individual "see." To help each individual understand, appreciate and value continuous improvement. This means to share knowledge, information and methods. Show them how to identify the issues and develop ideas to improve. It means allowing time for individuals to train and then to put that training into action through small groups and kaizen events.

Supplying A Need

The next definition is "a system supplying a need." The organization needs a robust system to generate ideas, projects and to sustain improvements. But it should also be designed to contribute to employee learning. This can be done very creatively through the design of the kaizen program.

Make no mistake. There is an absolute need for individuals to be a part of something big, to become intertwined in the day-to-day tasks as well as take part in daily improvements. This is not only a need of the employee to feel empowered and appreciated but also a real need for management. The minds on the floor are valuable, priceless even.

A robust continuous improvement training program, a kaizen suggestion system along with recognition programs and succession planning are vital in continuous improvement culture.

There is also a need for a continuous improvement team. This team is not only in charge of recurrent training, engaging and keeping interest high, but it also is responsible for "performing routine maintenance" to the system design.

Employees need recurrent teaching. It's essential for them to hear the continuous improvement message frequently. That said, they do not just need to "hear" it, they need to see it as well.

Most would not hesitate to implement a torque audit to ensure tooling is reaching its maximum potential or a PM program to prevent a machine from breaking down. Likewise a "PM program" must be in place for employees so they do not "breakdown" or become complacent in their jobs.

In a continuous improvement-driven organization, the last thing you want to see is employees just coming in to do the same old grind.

Lean Continuous Improvement empowers the employee by providing opportunity. It makes training, support and systems available to the employee for job enlargement. It creates excitement and cultivates passion. It transforms an employee's responsibility from performing a process to sustaining and improving it, from coming in and doing the bare minimum to going above and beyond.

Continuous Improvement is a service program and should be dedicated to elevating the minds and talents of everyone within the organization. It should be dedicated to helping employees by supplying the knowledge to create and the freedom to implement.

There is not truly a Lean Continuous Improvement Culture until every employee, at every level, uses continuous improvement practices and would not think of doing their jobs any other way.

Any organization will make great strides if they shift their mentality to service. Serve the people, invest in the people. The company will grow as the minds grow.

Chapter 8: Union's Perspectives on Lean

A lot of people are getting sick of hearing how good we have got it from politician all over the world. "The economy is booming." "Everybody loves Obama." "The stock market is up." "Everybody has a job." This is what our betters on Wall Street and the network news, in the think tanks and newspaper columns, say we should be grateful for. But then nobody we know feels lucky, or secure, or rich. So who's crazy?

If you are a young person contemplating the job market, even someone with a college degree, everyone tells you "there are no careers." You are supposed to be thrilled by the fact that you will jump from job to job for the rest of your life; it's called "flexibility" or "being entrepreneurial." Many people in their twenties are trying to get used to the idea that they will spend the rest of their lives working temporary or boring, routine jobs with no chance to use their brain or get a promotion; much less buy a house.

According to the Bureau of Labour Statistics' 1996 projections, the fastest growing occupations in the next millennium will be personal home health aides, manicurists and correction officers. Even jobs once considered "professional" university teaching, engineering, computer programming are being transformed into part-time, temporary occupations where today's skills may be useless tomorrow.

"It's fine if you don't mind being an alienated youth person for the rest of your life," said one graduate school dropout turned part-time secretary turned socialist. "But if you wanted to have a family, you feel cheated." Some people scrounge up loans and financial aid to go to University just to have a place to hide out for a few years, before they enter this dismal rat race. Just about no one in this generation believes they will collect Social Security when they retire. If you are an older person with a job, you feel cheated too. Your workload is bigger than ever, you may have a weird new "flexible" work schedule, the lay-off axe is always hanging over your head, and your wages haven't kept up with inflation. Lots of people hate the forced overtime; others grab as much as they can, to keep up with their bills. Management is always coming up with some brilliant new program at work to get you to "buy in" to working harder. The results are increased heart disease, repetitive stress injuries and lots of depression.

To make it worse, at the very time that social services like good health care, unemployment benefits, Social Security pensions, welfare, and childcare are needed more than ever; governments are cutting or dismantling these programs. Just when we are working so hard that we have less time to care for our children and parents, more and more of this burden is falling on individual families.

So, the 2000s has been a decade of intense economic contradictions. On one hand, profits are at their highest level since the 1970s. Corporations are doing better today than at any time in the last thirty years and most ordinary working people are doing worse. What's wrong with this picture?

Part of the reason we are hurting is the changes employers have made in the way they organize work, and therefore in the way they make us work. The new work system, which got its start in the auto industry in Japan but is now used all over the world, is called lean production.

Lean production is the cutting edge of the corporations' and governments' attempt to reorganize social life. Lean Production judges everything and everyone on the basis of speed and productivity. If anything or anyone does not fit the needs of speed and productivity, they are disposable; whether they are a good, service or whole categories of people.

The heart of lean production is reorganizing work to cut costs. Sometimes it goes under names like "Total Quality Management" or "team concept" or "reengineering," but we prefer the more accurate title "Management by Stress." Any worker is familiar with the "slogan of the month" new programs management comes up with to increase productivity. While they say they want workers' "input," what they're really looking for is more "output."

Bosses have been reorganizing the way we work ever since the beginnings of industrial capitalism. In the early twentieth century, it was called "Taylorism," after Fredrick Winslow Taylor, the father of Scientific Management. Taylor urged employers to do time-motion studies of workers, concentrate all planning work in the hands of managers, and give workers detailed instructions on simple and repetitive tasks. Henry Ford combined Taylor's ideas with the assembly line to increase the speed of work even more. Later, automation and now computerization increased productivity (output per worker) even further. Lean production is the latest version of these schemes to get more work out of fewer people.

From management's point of view, the beauty of lean production is "eliminating waste" getting rid of "excess" activities, materials and workers. The only problem is, their definition of "waste" includes most things that make work life bearable, like breaks, or a reasonable pace, or a set work schedule, or a decent pay cheque, or job security. To get the greatest bang for the buck, lean production stresses workers to the limits of their capacities, through;

1. Speed-up, plain and simple; just work faster, or do more jobs, or do the same with fewer people.
2. Deskilling break the jobs down so they take little time to learn. This saves money because higher paid skilled workers can be replaced with lower paid unskilled workers.
3. "Multi-skilling" really multi-tasking. Doing more jobs, usually of the deskilled variety.
4. Contracting out or privatization of work previously done by unionized workers.
5. Use of temporaries, part-timers, and contract workers.
6. More flexibility for management in setting hours and tasks.

7. Cracking down on absenteeism and eliminating replacements for people who are absent or retire.

Employers have introduced lean methods in all walks of life, from phone companies to health care to coal mines. Hospitals have turned nurses' work over to unlicensed aides; universities replace tenured professors with part-timers and use e-mail and the Web to increase workloads.

The auto industry is where lean production first hit the United States, so we will use it as an example. An assembly-line worker in a traditional auto plant could perform his or her assigned tasks in say 45 seconds of the minute the car body moved through his or her workstation. This allowed the assembler to work faster for a period of time ("work up the line") in order to create an unofficial break. In a lean production plant, this is impossible. Work is structured so that the worker requires 58 seconds to complete the tasks; management's aim is for everyone to work continuously. One autoworker described working in a lean factory as "eight hours of aerobic activity each day." Today at auto plants, workers must constantly struggle with their bosses to get bathroom breaks, which management labels as "wasted time."

Management by stress has also made the work process tighter. Manufacturers have eliminated large inventories of parts; instead, parts are delivered "just in time," so the pressure is on the supplier plants. They have laid out the assembly line so that each phase of the production process is tightly synchronized with the next. Such a "lean" system means they can reduce the number of supervisors needed to directly observe workers; which is not all bad. But the system itself creates the pressure to never make a mistake.

Then management applies another type of pressure for workers to actively participate in speeding up their own jobs, through task forces and teams. It is no longer enough for workers to come to work and do their jobs; they need to become "partners in production." Management calls this "empowerment." Many union activists call it "cutting your own throat."

The introduction of new, expensive technology like computers, a feature of the lean workplace, does not necessarily mean that workers are gaining more skills. Contrary to what the futurists have predicted, new technology today often means deskilling. Through "expert programs," or "foolproof" electronic eyes to do inspection, the judgment calls have been taken away from us "fools" and turned over to the machines. Your job is to keep up with the machine. Lean production cuts costs not only by reorganizing the workplace but also by sending a lot of the work someplace else, through contracting out, outsourcing and privatization. Lower-paid, non-union workers now do the jobs previously done by relatively well paid, unionized workers.

Public employees; postal workers, teachers, transit workers, hospital workers, social workers, sanitation workers and others are among the most likely to be unionized. When federal, state and local governments have given private firms contracts to provide services; the results have been disastrous for both public employees and the public at large. Not only are the wages and working conditions at the private contractors much worse, but the contractors often reduce services to boost their profits. It is not uncommon for cities with privatized garbage collection to see frequency drop from twice a week to one a week.

Unions have traditionally attempted to "remove labour from competition" by bargaining for uniform wages and working conditions within a company and industry. Privatization is one way to create competition among workers-giving work to the lowest bidder. Another way is through two-tier workforces, where new-hires are paid substantially less and are put on a different track where they will never catch up.

Whether a second tier exists in a particular workplace or not, two-tier is certainly the case in the workforce as a whole. The top tier is a shrinking number of permanent (till you are laid off), full-time, decent-paying (but less so) jobs. The second-tier jobs are increasing rapidly, pay less, are temporary, maybe part-time, and almost never union. What the two tiers have in common is that in both of them, life on the job is more stressful than ever. The second-tier workers are disproportionately women, young people, African-Americans and Latinos or those forced out of their former good jobs.

In public universities and colleges, for example, close to half of all classes are taught by adjunct faculty part-timers who are paid far less than full-timers and usually have to hold several teaching jobs at once. In some public sector workplaces, the second tier is workfare workers. Welfare recipients who receive less than the minimum wage and can be denied their meagre benefits for any minor offense are cleaning parks, mopping floors in government buildings and filing in government offices; work previously done by union members. Government policies have aided and abetted the corporations' drive to increase competition among workers. Workfare was created not just so that politicians could brag about putting "freeloaders" to work; it was a way to push hundreds of thousands of people into the workforce, and thus keep wages for those bottom-of-the-heap jobs low. Legislation that deregulated the trucking, airlines and telecommunications industries intensified competition and thus encouraged employers to reorganize work and undermine job security. North American Free Trade Agreement (NAFTA) made millions of workers fear their employers would move to Mexico and therefore made them willing to give concessions or vote no in a union drive.

Chapter 9: Why Lean?

Union's Perspectives on Lean Continues!

Why have corporations and government embraced lean?

Union Leaders have two answers. First, they say that our bosses are acting irrationally when they pay low wages, cut jobs, and intensify competition among workers. Most other top union officials argue plaintively that corporations and governments are shooting themselves in the foot by pursuing this "low road" (wage cutting) to competitiveness. Second, they argue that corporations are simply "greedy." Rather than being satisfied with a "reasonable" return on their investments, corporations attempt to maximize profits at the expense of the rest of us.

Union Leaders would like to convince employers to take the "high road." They should stop fighting unions. They should pay decent wages and realize that a good union, one with "partnership" as a policy, will help institute a "high-performance workplace," one with greater productivity, quality, and therefore profits. According to some Union Leaders "Common Sense Economics for Working Families. The Top 10 Myths about the Economy"; "When wages grow, consumers spend more; business invests more in efficiency and productivity increases. This leads to higher wages and economic growth and the cycle continues." What is wrong with this scenario? "Investing in efficiency and productivity" equals lean production and that means layoffs and lower wages for workers, not more jobs and higher wages.

Most union leaders seem to be caught in a time warp on this question; they did like to go back to the 1950s when U.S. corporations' dominance over their competitors allowed both workers' incomes and profits to grow together. Their belief in the possibility of a "win-win" solution where both workers and employers benefit has led them to embrace various forms of labour-management cooperation. Under various labels; Quality Circles, Team Concept, etc. Union leaders have offered their support in management's bid for competitiveness. Union leaders have agreed to cooperate with management to get workers to work harder and longer for less, in the hope that these givebacks might save jobs.

Many workers have had the same hopes and have agreed to these schemes. They may know the boss is out to screw them, but still feel they have to cooperate in the loss of work rules in the hope that management will not close their plant, or contract out their work.

Of course, the embrace of labour-management cooperation has not produced either job security or wage increases. In fact, cooperation schemes have helped pave the way for lean production's spread across workplaces. By giving up the protections of clear contractual language on job categories, for example, and by signing on to mandatory "teams" and the like, some unions have helped create a workplace environment where workers actively participate in implementing lean production. It's no longer enough to do the job to get paid; workers are expected to use peer pressure and contribute their ideas to speed up and cut jobs.

Union Leader's economics helps the labour officialdom justify its strategy of labour-management cooperation. The strategy of "jointers" has many benefits for the labour bureaucracy; it creates many more full-time union positions to administer labour-management cooperation schemas and it provides an alternative to the mobilization of rank and file workers which could endanger the political and social position of the officialdom.

Unfortunately, Union Leaders advocates that; there are no "win-win" situations for both capitalists and workers. Capitalism creates a "zero-sum game" every gain for capitalists in competitiveness and profitability comes at the costs of workers' wages and working conditions.

It is true that one group of workers may gain short-term job security as a result of cooperating with their bosses; however, these gains must come at the expense of other workers (now called "the competition") and competition among workers has long-term consequences. When workers in different companies, workplaces or even departments are pitted against one another, the race to the bottom is on. The temporary winners will soon be asked for more givebacks as the next round of competition begins.

The conflict between workers and employers is built into the basic structure of capitalism. Workers create the vast majority of accumulated wealth. In the words of "Solidarity Forever": "It is we who ploughed the prairies; built the cities where they trade; Dug the mines and built the workshops; endless miles of railroad laid." Yet the capitalists control this productive wealth (land, machinery, offices, etc.). They set up work in a way that ensures workers will create goods and services far beyond the value of what we take home in wages and benefits. It is this "unpaid labour" that is the source of all profit in capitalist society.

Without the workers, no profits, no huge salaries for managers and executives, no new investment. To increase profits, capitalists must get workers to work as long and as hard as possible for as little as possible. Our wages are their costs. Any improvement for us, in pay or working conditions, must come out of profits and vice versa. Because the bosses' gains are the workers' losses, the interests of capitalists and workers are fundamentally opposed. Try as they might and many have no one can wish away this basic conflict of interests.

The driving forces of capitalism profitability and competition-make the conflict between workers and capitalists continuous and irreconcilable. What will bring the greatest return on their investment drives every major decision capitalists make. Profits decide what is produced (tanks or deodorant), where it is produced (Indonesia or the U.S.) and how to produce it (hand tools or automated machinery). The needs of consumers, the environment, workers do not matter. As long as profits are made, capitalists do not care whether their factories pollute the air and water or working people suffer from unemployment, poverty and workplace diseases. The infamous cost-benefit decision that led to the production of the Ford Pinto-profits were projected to be much greater than the money that could be lost to the lawsuits of the bereaved is one example of the perverse logic of profitability. Regardless of the desires of individual managers or owners, for capitalists the bottom line is the only line.

It's not greed that drives capitalists to get the biggest bang for their buck (although greed there is aplenty). Competition is the disciplining force that forces each and every capitalist to minimize costs and maximize returns. Lowering prices is the main way companies compete with one another. The company that can offer the same quality product for a lower price (or a higher quality product for the same price) wins that company increases its share of the market and makes more profits. If management decides to raise their workers' wages or improve their conditions, the company's costs go up. The company will not be able to offer its product for a competitive price; it will lose market share and make less profit than its competitors. No one will invest in a business that is not making a good profit, so the company's source of money for new investments needed to buy more efficient machines and computers-dries up. Any capitalist who loses money or even one who makes a lower profit rate than others faces the possibility of going bankrupt.

The cut-throat nature of capitalist competition can be clearly seen in the anti-trust trial against Microsoft. In their quest to dominate the computer software market, Microsoft's executives have used every available means to eliminate potential competitors. Microsoft's executives showed little concern for the fate of other corporate chieftains, much less the hundreds of thousands of workers whose livelihood was at stake. The Microsoft case also shows the real limits of government attempts to regulate competition. Only when other giant corporations (Sun, Netscape, America On-Line) find themselves harmed by "unfair competitive practices" does the government step in to "level the playing field."

Competition and the drive to maximize profits through the introduction of new technology spur capitalism to long periods of economic growth. The twenty-five years after the Second World War were such a long capitalist boom. But ironically, the very things capitalists do to remain competitive, especially the replacement of workers with new technology, eventually lead to falling profits on new investments and to long periods of economic stagnation and crisis like the one that began in the early 1970s and is just now ending. This is because the introduction of new technology has contradictory effects on the capitalist system. When each individual company invests in new technology, that company improves its competitive position vis a vis the others. But at the same time, the rising cost of technology lowers the rate of profit for all the capitalists. What had been a logical and rational decision for each competitor ultimately leads to lower profits for all, and thus a crisis for the whole system.

Falling profits intensify competitive pressures on capitalists to cut costs at the expense of workers. As profits fell sharply in the early 1970s, capitalists began to search for ways to lower costs. At first, it didn't occur to managers to break the union contracts that had helped provide stability for so long. Chrysler set the ball rolling when it asked the UAW for concessions in 1979. When other companies saw that union leaders were willing to say yes, they began an offensive against unions-and non-union workers that continues to this day. Lean production marks the high point of corporate attacks on unions and government slashing of social benefits.

Taylorism, Fordism, and now lean production do make sense for capitalists and lean production seems to be bringing them positive results. Combined with the elimination of the least profitable companies through bankruptcies and mergers, lean production's reduction of wages and increases in productivity have brought some increase in corporate profits since the early 1990s. Capitalists and their representatives in government are keenly aware that the only way they can continue this recovery of profitability is to continue and deepen lean production.

Chapter 10: Lean and Unions Can Co-exist

Over my career one question that I have been asked repeatedly is, "Does lean work in a Union environment?"

I have found that people ask this based on a couple of reasons. One reason is they see the success of lean at Toyota and they are a non-union company. The other reason is the company they are working in either is a union environment that is fighting the lean implementation or a non-union environment.

The answer is absolutely yes lean can work and has worked in union environments. I have worked in several union facilities with different unions. It all comes down to how management approaches lean and how willing the union is to accepting what they are hearing. Of course, how management approaches it can greatly affect how unions might accept it.

When I started working for an automotive supplier the facility had just changed leadership. The change was due to the previous leadership doing almost every possible illegal act to prevent a union from coming in to the non-union facility. The facility spent 5 years in litigation before everything was settled and a vote was scheduled to take place. Over that time we had started implementing lean and were having great success. Year over year improvements, increased profitability, and increased moral. When it came to time to vote the union was voted down 420 to 4. Quite a resounding number. I believe lean was part of the reason. We were getting employees engaged and showing they mattered. We didn't want them "checking their brains at the door." This was a case of how lean showed the respect for the people so they didn't feel a need to unionize.

When I worked at one of the leading automotive part supplier in the UK, 3 of the 4 facilities were unionized. All three of the unionized facilities were represented by different unions. In one location, the leadership team was going on a benchmark trip to kind of "kickoff" deeper lean implementation. The plant leadership invited the union leadership to come with them on the trip. The facility they were going to benchmark was represented by a union also. During the trip both the plant and union leadership toured the site and saw the work they had been doing. At one point, the plant leadership invited the union leaders from our plant to have a private discussion with their union leaders to understand the benefits, hurdles, and lessons learned from implementing lean in the union environment. It was extremely powerful. It showed the union leaders that the plant leaders didn't want to influence their decision. By the end of the trip the union leaders were 100% onboard with plant leadership. The union leaders were the ones that communicated to their people about going down the lean path. It allowed for a very open and a much easier implementation and relationship with the union.

At the same company, another facility had union representing the workers. The workers had went on strike a few years earlier, so there was still some animosity left over from that time. The plant leadership went in and said this is what we are doing without any discussion of how lean would impact the people and the work with the union. At first, the people resisted. This caused some work not to move as fast and also a confrontation or two. Eventually, the site lean leader did a good job of showing results and bridged the gap between the union and the leadership. There was still an air of mistrust between the union and the plant leadership. One thing both could agree upon was the economy was heading in the tank and they both better try something different to save as many jobs as they could. It isn't the best way to have a working relationship, but as Dr. House says, "The why doesn't matter." Hopefully, the facility has mended those bridges by now.

My personal belief is that if you are implementing lean well and truly respecting people then a union won't be necessary, but if you don't the union is a way for the people to gain a voice.

Chapter 11: Managing in a Unionized Workplace

Imagine that you have just walked into the office and you see that one of your people, Mike, is sitting at his desk without any work to do. So, you ask him to help another team member finish an urgent job.

Mike refuses, saying that taking on a different role, even for a day, is not allowed under the union contract. He tells you that, if you want him to do another team member's work, then you must talk to the union, as it's not part of his job description.

You have only been in this role for a week, and now you are stressed and confused about what you can and can't ask your people to do!

This might seem like an extreme example to many people, but it demonstrates that it can be complicated to manage unionized workers, especially if you are new to this type of working environment. In this chapter, we will look at the complexities and challenges of managing in a unionized workplace.

The content of this chapter is a general guide only. Union rights vary widely depending on your region, state, and country, and, most importantly, on the agreement that your organization has in place with unionized workers. Please seek the guidance of your human resources department or an employment lawyer if you need help with specific laws or situations.

Also, different unions and different union officials have different approaches. Some unions may be very traditional, confrontational, and even in some countries violent; while others may be more flexible and supportive of the long-term success of the organization.

A reminder of the history of Union

Before workers began banding together, working conditions were often very poor. People could work long hours for low pay, and with few benefits. They may even have worked in factories that were dangerous, and where workplace accidents were common. In fact, workers had few rights at all!

In response to such poor conditions, workers began joining together to pressure their employers to improve their work environment; they began forming unions.

Unions have a long history. In the U.K. people started forming during the Industrial Revolution, but these didn't become legal until 1867. Unions emerged in the U.S. in the 1870s.

A union is a group of workers who have come together to make collective decisions about their work and their working conditions. Union is democratic; members elect their leaders through a voting process. Through collective bargaining, these leaders negotiate with their employer over wages, working conditions, safety, hours, and other benefits, on behalf of their members.

Unions are based on the idea that a group is stronger than an individual. As a result of early union bargaining there are a variety of benefits that workers can enjoy today (depending on their location), such as a minimum wage, workplace safety standards, overtime, health care, and an eight-hour workday. As a result of unions, union members often receive higher pay and get better benefits than equivalent non-unionized workers.

In some cases, unions can be highly politicized; and they may be in alliance with specific political parties.

When an employer refuses to negotiate with a union, or when the two can't reach a compromise, the union may go on strike. In some countries, strikes are often the last resort as workers may lose pay as a result of strike; however, in others, union strikes are common and can be violent, resulting in injuries and even deaths.

In many cases, members pay monthly or yearly dues to their union, and the union uses these funds to pay workers a salary during a strike. It also uses these funds to provide other benefits, such as discounts on other services, legal consultations, and additional training.

Prevalence

Membership in unions varies widely, depending on the country you live in, local employee legislation, and the extent to which unions have power to protect employees.

Union Rights Around the World

The rights of unionized workers can vary widely depending on your industry, region, and country. Laws, rules, and regulations can also be incredibly complex. These rights are constantly changing, as state and national governments enact laws to protect or diminish the rights of union workers.

A good example of the global differences between unions is the "closed-shop policy." A closed shop is a form of union security agreement, where an organization agrees to hire union members only, and employees must be part of the union to remain employed. In the U.S. and U.K., closed shops are illegal.

Challenges

A number of challenges can arise when managing in a unionized environment. One of the biggest is flexibility or, rather, the lack thereof. Union workers often work set hours, and they must take a certain number of breaks during the day, no matter how heavy or how light the workload. This means that it can be difficult for managers to bring in new ways of working, as all changes need to be agreed with the union first.

This inflexibility also affects cross-training. Many unions stipulate that a worker has one role, and that they must not carry out any task that falls outside their job description. This can be frustrating for employers, especially when there are seasonal changes in work volume, and when workers are off sick. Most non-unionized organizations have a flexible workforce that can rearrange tasks depending on the company's needs, but this is often not the case with a unionized workforce.

Communication can be a challenge with union workers. Some union contracts require most, if not all, communication to go through union representatives, or at least be agreed with them in advance. This can mean that your team and union representatives don't include you in all discussions, which can be a real hindrance in building trust and credibility with your team. Other unions will require communications to be delivered to team members jointly, by yourself and the union representative. The main drawback of this is the extra time that it can take to communicate with your team.

Union contracts can also inhibit the effectiveness of a team or department, especially when people take advantage of the system. For example, many union contracts state that employees can have a set number of absences, or sick days, within a six-month period, before management penalizes them. Some workers take advantage of this, and take every sick day that they are entitled to, every six months.

The problem is that you can't fire these problem employees, and it can take years to prove that they are taking advantage of the system.

More subtly, a desire for "fairness," when seen as meaning "equal provision of benefits to everyone at the same level" as opposed to "fair reward for hard work," works against the customized approaches to compensation , motivation, and job enrichment that underpin job satisfaction and high performance.

Worryingly, unions can institutionalize conflict in the workplace, where union officials may think that they need to be seen to "stick up for members" to justify membership fees.

These challenges can be frustrating, but they underscore the importance of having a strong, trusting relationship with your union.

Although there are many challenges to managing in a unionized workplace, there can also be benefits. For example, you negotiate with a set group of people who are elected representatives of the workforce, meaning that you can come to an agreement on changes to terms of employment relatively quickly. They can also help you pinpoint and deal with issues that are upsetting people and reducing performance.

Strategies for Managing a Unionized Workforce

Despite the challenges, it is possible to develop and maintain a good working relationship with union officials.

1. Know the Law, Know Your Contracts, and Know Your History.

As we mentioned earlier, the laws and rules that govern unionized work are complex, and they vary widely depending on the union involved, as well as your state, region, and country.

It's essential that you become familiar with the union laws and rules that directly affect your organization and team. It's even more important that you know your team members' contracts, inside and out. The union and individuals will refer to the contract often in negotiations, and even during day-to-day work. The more familiar you are with their terms, the more effectively you'll be able to respond to questions or challenges.

It's also important to know the history of the recent relationship between the organization and unions. What have relations been like in the past, and, in particular, are there any points of special sensitivity that you need to be aware of?

2. Become Partners.

It's important to approach the union as a business partner, not as an adversary. You want to work with it, not against it; and when you take this approach, everyone can benefit. One of the ways that you can do this is to communicate openly and share ideas.

For example, imagine that you are having trouble with one team member who is consistently late. You have tried several strategies to try to get through to this person, and none have worked. In most cases, the union only hears of this when you are ready to fire the employee; however, imagine instead that you tell the union representatives about the problem. They can work with you to turn around this team member's behaviour, and they may also be able to provide assistance that you can't. For instance, if the person is often late because of day-care issues, the union might be able to secure reliable day-care for this employee.

Good partnerships are built on strong working relationships and these relationships take time to build. Put time into establishing trust with everyone on your team, including union representatives.

Next, build good relationships by spending time with your team outside of work. This could include work socializing, or even volunteer days, where everyone on the team volunteers for a social project in the community.

Another positive strategy is to share important information as soon as you reasonably can. Tell union representatives about upcoming changes or breaking news early, to give them a chance to brush up on the issues. That way, they will be prepared to answer questions from members. When you give them a heads up, it builds trust and establishes a practice of open communication.

When you have a good partnership with union representatives, you can ask for their help in solving disciplinary issues. A good example is the situation we described earlier, where people are consistently using all of their allowable sick days.

3. Focus on the Positive

Much of the time, managers only interact with union representatives when there is a problem. This means that these relationships are often built in stressful, tense situations, and, as a result, there is often a lack of trust on both sides.

Foster a positive relationship with union representatives by working with them on strategies that reward positive behaviours, not punish negative ones.

For example, imagine that your current system penalizes your customer service team if calls run over seven minutes. You could create a positive incentive by rewarding team members who receive a good review from customers. This not only raises moral, but it also makes everyone in the union happier.

Remember, apart from negotiating compensation, the union's primary goals are the safety and happiness of its members. When you promote these positive objectives, everyone is more willing to work together.

4. Show Respect

Remember that the union fulfils an important role for employees.

It's easy for managers or outsiders to fall into the trap of thinking that the union is always wrong, or that union representatives deliberately make things difficult for managers. Respect the positive changes that the union is trying to make, and keep this good intention at the forefront of any conversation or negotiation.

This chapter discusses successfully dealing with unionized workers in a positive way. There are some situations where good relations can break down, for example, when unions have decided that a strike is the only available course of action. Please seek the guidance of an employment lawyer, or of your human resources department, for help in these situations.

Chapter 12: Example of Unionized Environment

U. S. Healthcare is a growing, consolidated industry with billions flowing into its coffers and desperately in need of skilled labour. It's the kind of organizing target U.S. unions have not seen for some time.

While unions have already achieved a density of 21 percent in hospitals over the last two decades, by some estimates well above the national average; they will need more to tame the lean and mean regime brought on by a radical reorganization of hospital work.

Today's hospitals are big business, run like factories and clustered in growing corporate systems, the result of 597 mergers from 2000 through 2009. Almost three-quarters of private hospitals belong to such systems, concentrated in urban areas. For-profit hospitals are on the rise, intensifying the competition for private and public insurance revenues.

Whatever "non-profit" hospitals once were, today they are profit-seeking businesses, paying CEOs as much as $1.4 million a year. A survey of hospital executives found that their highest priority was "operating profit margin."

Competition and cost-cutting pressures have led hospital managers to turn to lean production methods straight from the Toyota playbook; lean manufacturing, Six Sigma, and supply chain strategies aimed at greater efficiencies.

As with all such management-by-stress systems, "efficiency" means greater output with fewer workers. In America's hospitals this has brought staff reductions, more outsourcing and agency workers at all levels, increasing standardization of treatment, and reorganization of work.

Outsourcing has long impacted the ancillary workforce, as food service, telephone provision, and other services are farmed out. The use of agency workers has become common for nurses, too. As short-staffing has made patient care more difficult and stressful, protection of quality care and patients' rights have become prime union goals.

Standardization and reorganization of work are enabled by investments in new technology. Real assets per worker have grown at 5 percent or more a year since 1990; about three times the pace during the 1980s. Some of this investment is in digital labour-controlling programs such as Clinical Decision Support Systems, a program that standardizes treatment, now used in nearly two-thirds of hospitals nationwide in the U.S.

Even electronic medical records, a seemingly neutral advance, increase standardization of care and provide the means to reduce the workforce.

Although the resulting pressures affect nurses most directly, they impact the entire workforce as cost-cutting pressures grow. This shows up in wage trends. Median weekly earnings, adjusted for inflation, have risen only slowly for the last 10 years; a mere three-tenths of 1 percent a year for support workers. Even nurses, whose pay is relatively decent, saw only a half percent increase per year in real terms.

Unionized health care workers, of course, have done considerably better, with major contracts often producing 3-4 percent annual raises.

For nurses in particular, hospital work has become intense. The recession made matters worse, as more than half a million hospital jobs disappeared between 2007 and 2008, before recovering in 2010.

In addition, the shift of less ill patients to outpatient care, to cut costs, has meant that the remaining inpatients are sicker and require more time-consuming care.

But because hospitals (except in California) aren't required by state law to cap the number of patients each nurse cares for, nurses are pressured to take more patients than they can handle, giving each less bedside time. Nurses unions, especially those affiliated with the new National Nurses United, have made nurse/patient ratios a central bargaining, organizing, and political issue.

As with all lean systems, hospital management demands greater workforce "flexibility." For nurses this means "floating," transferring a nurse temporarily from one ward to another. Nursing, however, is not a one-size-fits-all occupation. Nurses specialize. Floating ignores this fact, so, it too has become a key bargaining issue.

Unions have fought to limit overtime because it is another central aspect of lean flexibility as well as a way to reduce staff. The battle is often legislative. While a campaign to win federal limits failed, nine states have passed laws limiting nurses' overtime, due to union efforts. Most restrict work beyond 12 hours, but in New Jersey after eight hours.

Challenging work intensification has, of course, met fierce resistance from profit-seeking hospital managements. As a result the use of strikes and strike threats by health care unions has increased, even while strikes by most unions have dropped sharply.

One-third of the 91 contracts negotiated with hospitals in 2009 and 2010 involved explicit strike threats. Eight actually led to a strike five of which were led by a nurses union.

As President Obama's health care law reduces Medicare payments to hospitals, it will increase pressures to restrain wages and intensify work (while pouring billions into the insurance industry).

As some 34 million people gain either public or private insurance, the hospital industry will grow. But the aggressive for-profit chains will skim the healthiest from the private insurance market and specialize in the most lucrative services, leaving the mass of Medicare and Medicaid patients for the "nonprofits." These will see more cost pressures.

Given the complexity of the multi-payer system, much of the new money flowing to hospitals will go to administration. Administrative expenses already average 23 percent of costs, far higher than in national or single-payer health care systems in other developed nations.

Bookkeeping costs cut into care-giving. With millions of new forms to process and claims to argue over, administrative costs will be an increased drain on hospitals and thus a pressure on the workforce.

Hospital growth could mean union growth, and lean production pressures certainly give workers more incentives to organize.

But unions oriented to partnership with employers are unlikely to attract the workers who are feeling those pressures. Nor are they likely to win concessions from aggressive managements.

Instead, the dual patients' advocate, workers' advocate approach taken by a number of unions, especially the nurses, is far more likely to make the breakthrough this new situation offers.

Chapter 13: People Systems in a Lean Transformation

It's a given that lean transformations emphasize worker participation, but too often the role of the human resources organization is overlooked.

It surprises me how little folks actually think about the people side of lean. They don't really step back and look at all the components of the management system and ask what needs to change in their HR practices to drive lean transformation.

That can be a costly mistake. When a friend of mine worked at Toyota, He saw how human resources plays an essential role in the Toyota Production System. It became clear to him that a big gap exists in many organizations between lean thinking and the HR management systems.

Employee selection, compensation, promotion, and retention practices; all activities that typically land in HR's wheelhouse need to support the transformation to a lean enterprise. Instead, these systems tend to be based on traditional personnel beliefs and practices that often fail to promote the kinds of thinking and practices that support lean.

You want behaviour to change to bring about a successful lean outcome, but too often we see traditional organizations continuing to provide incentives for people not to change. For example, incentive programs that encourage employees to maintain high production volumes, boost revenue, and get ahead through individual effort may work at cross-purposes to the behaviours needed to achieve a lean transformation. Companies need to encourage team-based behaviour to support the learning organization. All the things an organization does should be aligned with the behaviour we want to see. Your people systems should directly support the kind of team-based, problem solving culture we want to achieve.

Lean HR Competencies

Adapting traditional HR management systems to support lean isn't easy. For instance, when we work with a client on lean transformation, a key area of focus is the organization's core competencies. As is often the case, these core skills tend to be wholly functional, instead of the kind of team-oriented abilities that support lean success.

You have to define the gaps between the organization's current competencies and those that need to be developed for lean success. Once you have defined the gaps, then HR has certain tools at its disposal to begin closing them. Among them are:
1. Align specifications for a new job with a set of lean behaviours.
2. Reorganize the HR structure to support the model of leader as teacher.
3. Keep lean behaviours in mind when assessing and selecting the right person for a job.

4. Emphasize the applicant's potential to fit in with the team in the employee selection process.
5. Establish a new definition of what good work is that incorporates lean behaviours.
6. Include how well a person engages with and understands their role as part of the team in their performance evaluation.
7. Modify the promotion process to support lean behaviours such as coaching and teaching on the part of supervisors and managers.

Although developing employees is essential to any lean transformation, traditional HR management tends to place little emphasis on managers' performance as teachers and coaches. How well managers are developing people in the organization is very important in lean. Traditional compensation systems typically reward management only for bottom-line results. Managers should be rewarded for their ability to execute talent management and development. As with everything else in lean, we need to think about people systems in a different way.

When working on lean engagement you should map the organization's strengths and weaknesses. Then identify which competencies need to be developed to ensure a successful lean transformation. These often include:
1. A quality first orientation.
2. An emphasis on customer service.
3. A team orientation.
4. More effective communications.

Participants should learn how the most critical components of people systems affect lean behaviours and competencies. One of the big contributions this makes to any lean transformation is the focus on these competencies and the need to involve HR early in the lean transformation.

Enlisting HR's participation in lean from the get-go is critical. Unfortunately, most companies tend to only seek HR's help when it's required to effect a change in policy or job descriptions. In my personal experience, it's the distinct minority of organizations where the HR organization is fully engaged in the lean transformation.

It's not only the younger, less mature organizations that fail to engage HR up front when embarking on a lean journey. I expect that in small, entrepreneurial companies, but it surprises me to find that is the case in many medium-to large-size companies.

Regardless of the size of the organization, leaving HR out of the lean loop until the eleventh hour can prove to be a crippling oversight. HR can help, but it also can hinder the changes to new ways of doing things.

You can't get there without making sure that your people systems are aligning with lean. The process of moving the organization from A to B cannot go well without changing the people processes. That is because the lean management system falls apart without appropriate people systems. This point can't be overly stressed. HR needs to be involved from the beginning, because HR is the keeper of the values of the organization. HR holds the keys to the People Systems car.

Both HR professionals and senior leaders and professionals from other organizational disciplines organizational design, organization effectiveness, change agents, process engineers, and lean leaders are encouraged to align HR policies and practices with your effort to create a lean culture of continuous improvement.

Chapter 14: Lean and Employee Engagement

Engaged employees perform better, are more motivated, are less likely to quit and are more likely to be good ambassadors for the firm and its brand. They also tend to exhibit a higher state of well-being and have fewer sick days, according to a recent research.

Unfortunately, engaged employees are not that commonplace. Over the last decade or so, my favourite question to ask audiences when I do public speaking has always been this one.

What percentage of your intellectual potential, your creativity and your passion do you think your organization gets from you?

I ask people to raise their hands if they think it's more than eighty percent, between eighty and fifty percent, between fifty and twenty percent or less than twenty percent. Usually the last two categories get the majority of hands by far.

A recent report on employee engagement, based on a survey with more than eight thousand participants worldwide, only about one third of employees are fully engaged in their work. A 2013 Workforce Survey with more than 34,000 participants in large and midsized firms found similarly discouraging findings, with only 35% employees highly engaged in their jobs. This is a sad state of affairs.

What do we mean by Employee Engagement?

There are two key components of employee engagement; job satisfaction and job contribution. By job satisfaction we are referring to how much employees feel they are getting out of the job. Job contribution, on the other hand, specifies how much employees (feel they) are contributing at work. Thus my frequently-asked question above is about job contribution, not job satisfaction.

Based on surveying both job satisfaction and contribution, a recent report identifies the following levels of employee engagement.

1. **The Engaged:** High contribution and high Satisfaction.
2. **Almost Engaged:** Medium to high contribution and satisfaction.
3. **Honeymooners and Hamsters:** High satisfaction but low contribution.
4. **Crash and Burners:** High contribution but low satisfaction.
5. **The Disengaged:** Low contribution and satisfaction

This model of employee engagement makes it easier to understand how some people seem to coast and appear satisfied with their jobs, while others work very hard, but then suddenly quit in frustration.

It is worth noting that the percentage of Engaged Employees in this study varies significantly by geographical region (GCC stands for "Gulf Cooperation Council"):

India 58%
North America 60%
Australia and NZ 63%
South America 63%
GCC 66%
Europe 69%
China 78%

Factors that affect employee engagement

These numbers are difficult to decipher unless we can better understand what most affects job satisfaction and contribution. The survey identifies the following top job contribution drivers.
1. Clearer goals and expectations.
2. More resources.
3. Regular performance feedback.
4. Development opportunities and training.
5. A coach or a mentor other than my manager.
6. Better communication with my manager.
7. A better relationship with my co-workers

These drivers vary somewhat in importance based on engagement level and geographical region. The top job satisfaction drivers found by the survey were as follows:
1. More opportunity to do what I do best.
2. Career development opportunities and training.
3. More flexible job conditions.
4. More challenging work.
5. Improved cooperation.
6. Clearer goals and expectations.

7. Greater clarity about my own work preferences and career goals.
8. A better relationship with my manager.

Among these, "more opportunities to do what I do best" and "career development and training" rank high across every geographical region.

Perhaps the most striking finding in the survey is the correlation between trust and employee engagement. Ninety percent of Engaged Employees report that they trust their manager. For the Disengaged, that number is closer to fifty percent.

Another report identifies the following top drivers of sustainable employee engagement.

Leadership performance
1. Is effective at growing the business.
2. Shows sincere interest in employees' well-being.
3. Behaves consistently with the organization's core values.
4. Earns employees' trust and confidence.

Stress, balance and workload
1. Manageable stress levels at work.
2. A healthy balance between work and personal life.
3. Enough employees in the group to do the job right.
4. Flexible work arrangements.
5. Goals and objectives.

Employees understand
1. The organization's business goals.
2. Steps they need to take to reach those goals.
3. How their job contributes to achieving goals.

Managers
1. Assign tasks suited to employees' skills.
2. Act in ways consistent with their words.
3. Coach employees to improve performance.
4. Treat employees with respect.

Organization's image
1. Highly regarded by the general public.
2. Displays honesty and integrity in business activities.

It is understandable that the level of employee engagement varies across geographical regions, industries and organizations. After all, management practices and business cultures also vary widely.

Cause or effect? Reframing employee engagement

The way we frame a problem significantly impacts the types of solutions we are likely to look for. If we view employee engagement purely as an HR problem, we are more likely to launch projects to address deficiencies related to the satisfaction and performance factors above.

There is little doubt that such efforts will work, at least temporarily. For example, if your employees feel there is a lack of clear goals, frustrated over lack of training, or lack of trust in their managers, each of these issues can be addressed through specific remedies. Goals can be clarified, training budgets can be increased and managers can be coached or replaced.

I would suggest, however, that there is a different way to improve employee engagement. What if the drivers that affect engagement are merely symptoms of the overall mindset and management system in the company?

I recently had an interesting conversation with an executive who mentioned that her company did indeed have a significant problem with employee engagement. This, I learned, was having a negative impact on productivity.

While this is not surprising, my immediate reaction was to see if we could turn the relationship on its head. Instead of assuming that people are less productive because they are not engaged, what if people are less engaged because they are not experiencing being productive? In other words, perhaps they are not in a position where they feel they are contributing and fulfilling goals.

Because of the research that has already been done on factors that impact employee engagement, we do know something about the management practices and leadership behaviours that most affect employee engagement. To sustain employee engagement, an organization must deliver value to its customers through innovation and execution, but it must also provide fulfilment and growth for employees.

Can Lean improve Employee Engagement?

Lean is an approach to leadership and management that leverages the intellectual contribution of all employees to help organizations learn faster and create more value. We can describe Lean in terms of a mindset and a set of practices. The Lean Mindset views individuals as valuable learners and emphasizes leadership through teaching and continuous problem-solving.

Lean practices help organizations accelerate operations, remove waste, speed innovation, continuously improve performance, and help employees grow and develop. We often describe Lean as three systems in one.

1. An Operating System providing real-time transparency and accelerated execution.
2. An Organizational Learning System for continuous innovation and improvement.
3. A People System where managers help employees grow.

The People System aspect of Lean ensures that managers focus on facilitating learning and individual growth for employees. In a Lean Organization, managers function more like teachers than traditional bosses. Individual employees are on their own journey of continuous improvement, they are always learning.

The Organizational Learning System aspect of Lean involves all employees in continuously identifying and solving the problems that hinder the organization in fulfilling its goals and delivering value to customers. The emphasis on relentless improvement means that there are always new challenges to be overcome.

Lean as a Management System provides visibility and transparency in how work is conducted and where the bottlenecks are. From strategy deployment to daily execution, goals are made clear and employees are involved in setting them. The management system itself makes it clear what needs to be prioritized in order to reach the goals that have been set. This frees up managers from the job of assigning tasks and provides much more autonomy and flexibility for employees than in a traditional organization.

For all of these reasons and others I will omit due to space considerations, one would expect that organizations pursuing Lean would experience improved employee engagement.

The Need for Lean Leadership

Because the workforce is often already somewhat disengaged when the Lean effort starts, it may be difficult to get them involved initially, just as it would be difficult to embark on any new initiative. This does not account for ongoing difficulties, however over the years we have witnessed and heard of countless anecdotal reports of leaders who try to deploy Lean practices without themselves adopting a Lean mindset and corresponding leadership behaviours. They are still holding on to a traditional command-and-control mindset and are not comfortable with openly sharing information and granting more autonomy to employees.

I believe that this will not only limit the practical results of a Lean effort, it may also hurt employee engagement. Some managers and employees will disengage and feel like they are contributing even less, and others will work hard and have a bigger impact; however, they may burn out because their job satisfaction is not improving.

Lean Management can and will improve employee engagement only if leaders are willing to address the barriers to engagement that stem from their own behaviours. This means that they have to adopt a Lean Mindset as well. There can be no Lean transformation without Lean Leadership.

Chapter 15: Conclusion

Lean is designed to reduce the seven "deadly forms of waste": defects, overproduction, over processing, wasted motion, inventory (work in process), transport/handling and waiting. Addressing any or all of these can help operations run more efficiently and therefore, be more competitive which is in the long-term best interest of job security. But, in my experience as a former union member and internal change agent and currently as an organizational change consultant, Lean implementation in union environments can be tricky. Here's why.

1. Lean initiatives are typically introduced and championed by management leaders who sometimes see Lean as the silver bullet to solve their manufacturing problems. In their zest for addressing the ills of waste that plague their production lines, it's easy to skip the critical step of involving stakeholders in the decision to launch the initiative and the all-important planning of how.

2. Lipstick on a Pig. No matter how you try to paint it, lipstick on a pig is not pretty, and the members at the union hall aren't buying it. In locations where labour relations are strained and fostering distrust in management, union members may be quick to jump to the impression that Lean as a pig whose lipstick is designed to disguise intentions to gain efficiencies in order to eliminate jobs.

3. The Last to Know. Sensing labour leaders may be averse to Lean initiatives for a variety of reasons including number 2 above; management sometimes opts to avoid the perceived conflict and fails to bring their union counterparts into the discussion. Or, they decide to get just a little way down the road before sharing the information, or in organizations where labour and management leaders are not engaged in every day conversations about the business, it just may not occur to management to share the information. Whatever the cause, if management fails to engage with the union before the decision to implement is made, then they have waited too long. In almost every case this will mean news of plans to implement a Lean initiative will hit the plant floor before it hits the union hall and when that happens, union leaders may feel management has made them look foolish, out-of-the-loop and/or ineffective in their role of protecting jobs. As a result, union leaders may react by joining in the fracas and inadvertently give credibility to misinformation, making it ever more difficult to reverse course and build union and employee support for Lean.

All of these factors and more can pile on until it seems nearly impossible for Lean processes to work in unionized environments. But wait… before pulling the plug (and the rug out from under the operations that most need the efficiencies Lean can bring) leaders would be well served to consider these actions that can help Lean processes take root and flourish in even the most arid labour-management environments.

1. Management leaders interested in implementing Lean processes need to be sure that they don't leave would-be partners at the gate. So often, the issues that Lean seeks to address are the same factors that have irritated and plagued workers for years. They did like to resolve those problems as much, or more, as management. Where there is a shared interest in finding a better way to do work that eliminates waste and makes the operation and the work day run more smoothly, there is also an opportunity to embark on a Lean process together.

2. Lose the Lipstick. The best way for management to address workers' concerns about job loss is to confront the issue directly. If there will be job losses, management has a legal obligation to notify the union. If management plans to offer re-training and transfer opportunities in the event that efficiency gains may result in the need to re-define job classifications, that is likely to have ramifications for the collective bargaining agreement as well. Or, perhaps management believes efficiency gains will enable the firm to expand its business, creating new jobs. In any of these cases, the point is that direct, straightforward dialogue with union leaders about Lean's potential impact on jobs will equip them with information they need to address members' questions, and help prevent unfounded fears from spiralling out of control.

3. Sooner is Better. Many times, I have heard management leaders hesitate to communicate with their union counterparts because "We don't have all the information yet." Waiting until all the information

is known and decisions are at hand is simply too late. Once plans are fully baked, there is not much to discuss. Instead, management is setting up the classic "I tell; You react" chain of events that fosters adversarial relations. Letting labour leaders know what is being considered and why well before the actual decisions are made, can go a long way toward building trust and the foundation for a productive labour-management relationship.

My "Yes, of course answer in this book," response to the question of whether Lean can be implemented in union environments, hinges largely on management taking a proactive approach. It requires engaging union leaders in a frank discussion about Lean, and their motivation for considering it; exploring shared interests and concerns with labour leaders; discussing the potential implications on job security; and exchanging information early and often throughout the process.

While applying these approaches will create an opportunity to successfully introduce a Lean process, implementing it requires an on-going commitment to open communication and diligent efforts to involve union leaders and members in the process in meaningful ways. Successful Lean processes do not happen to employees and union leaders; they happen with them.

Good Luck!!